Copyright © 2019
Jorges Rhodes

All rights reserved. No part of this publication may be reproduced or distributed in any form or by any means, or stored in a database or retrieval system, without the prior written permission of the author, except where permitted by law.

Legal & Disclaimer

The information contained in this book is not designed to replace or take the place of any form of medication or professional medical advice. The information in this book has been provided for educational and entertainment purposes only.

The information contained in this book has been compiled from sources deemed reliable, and it is accurate to the best of the Author's knowledge. However, the Author cannot guarantee its accuracy and validity so cannot be held liable for any errors or omissions. Changes are periodically made to this book. You must consult your doctor or get professional medical advice before using any of the suggested remedies, techniques, or information in this book.

Upon using the information contained in this book, you agree to hold harmless the Author from and against any damages, costs and expenses, including any legal fees, potentially resulting from the application of any of the information provided by this guide. This disclaimer applies to any damages or injury caused by the use and application, whether directly or indirectly, of any advice or information presented, whether for breach of contract, tort, negligence, personal injury, criminal intent, or under any other cause of action.

You agree to accept all the risks of using the information presented inside this book. You need to consult a professional medical practitioner in order to ensure you are both able & healthy enough to participate in this program.

1 to 3 Year Smart Retirement Playbook "Retire Smart"

Contents

Introduction 3

Chapter 1: Retire Smartly 5

Factors to take into account to plan your retirement the right way 6

Chapter 2: Main Obstacles on the road to economic independence for the retirement stage 7

Chapter 3: Building Family Support for the Retirement Plan 10

Chapter 4: How do you gain financial independence to enjoy retirement? 11

Chapter 5: How to develop a savings plan for retirement? 16

Plan to build a retirement fund in 3 years 19

Chapter 6: Investment Strategy 23

Chapter 7: Mental Preparation for a new stage in you life. 25

Chapter 8: A 7 step system to end your procastination in retirement planning 27

Chapter 9: 10 Tips to get one financially stable 28

Chapter 10: 10 Gaps to avoid in preparation for retirement 29

Conclusion 31

Introduction

As society and the nature of work evolve, notions of retirement must also evolve, to adapt to new times and motivate people to work to build solid foundations for the future.

The pace of life led by the active population is so demanding that people only focus on meeting the needs of the moment. Sixty-six percent of Americans are concerned about having insufficient funds for their retirement. Some prefer to postpone the process, not thinking about how they will live when retirement comes. Others delay planning to save for their retirement and don't think about anticipating it because they think it's a luxury.

Waiting until you're 30 or 40 to start planning your retirement is late, but you can plan your retirement whenever you want. You may not be able to save enough to live a solvent life unless you use financial tools wisely.

With middle-aged people taking on life's biggest challenges, such as raising children, mortgages and car loans, saving becomes difficult because it requires a greater effort to contribute to the retirement plan.

The habit of the hour should be a motivating experience, rewarding, full of hope and security. It is the guarantee of living with financial freedom and enjoying a better quality of life. There is a tendency to think of the financial limitations involved in saving a high percentage of your income as a basis for the time of retirement. This thought delays the investment initiative and affects the quality of life you can have in your golden years.

Pension systems that maintain the highest standards of integrity, sustainability and adequacy make savings mandatory for the retirement fund. These systems include a percentage of savings on the part of the employer and another percentage on the part of the employee, according to the annual Melbourne Mercer Global Pension Index, which groups countries such as Australia, Denmark, and the Netherlands.

To be predictive and to think about how to live in our old age, it is planning for the arrival of a stage of our life, which inevitably approaches every day. It is the mentality of one who digs a hole before becoming thirsty.

Retire Smartly is a guide specially created for those who plan to retire and have financial stability quickly. It contains tips and useful information to help you make the transition from your professional life to retirement.

Having the rest and tranquility you desire after working tirelessly for many years of your life can be affected by the worry caused by the lack of money to meet the basics of your needs.

Rest, spend more time with your family and be able to do those things that you could not do for lack of time when you were working, is the dream of every worker who thinks at the time of retirement. For some people of retirement age, work is a necessary option to cover expenses; however, the sense of retirement is lost by limiting the enjoyment of this stage.

The concept of retirement has changed in recent times; previously the person retired and remained inactive and relaxed. Today, conditions exist to remain active and productive during the golden years. The foresighted and forward-looking person goes the extra mile and takes precautions for intelligent retirement.

Having difficulty covering your expenses is a problem, and borrowing is dangerous. A well-structured savings plan is the basis for freeing yourself from money worries.

Chapter 1
Retire Smartly

Smart retirement is about choosing the right financial instruments through a well-structured plan that provides real returns and ensures a happy retirement life.

Most systems make it mandatory to have a shared retirement plan, where the employer contributes a percentage in favor of the employee, and the employee contributes the other percentage, according to the labor legislation of each country.

There is also private retirement planning, in which a fund is established according to the savings capacity of each individual.

The reality is that employer-type retirement funds, while ensuring a benefit for the worker in retirement, limit the possibility of enjoying and resting, as they can only cover basic needs, mainly due to inflation.

Generally, the person who plans his retirement, wants to perform those activities that were limited by lack of time, such as traveling, visiting the family and spending more time with them, starting a new career or participating in a sport. However, he must secure the financial resources to enable the fulfillment of his dreams.

The so-called golden years are the most beautiful stage of life. In which you should feel satisfied to have raised a beautiful family, have a stable home, rest, and perform an activity that gives you more time to relax and share with loved ones. However, the obligations continue and having the worry of paying a mortgage or covering basic expenses, generates stress and anxiety.

It is advisable to think about private savings funds and other investment options that allow you to generate additional income. Likewise, professionals who have led an economically comfortable life need to maintain their lifestyle, and therefore have a retirement fund that meets their expectations.

The idea is to retire intelligently, to live well and not just survive. It is very convenient to start as early as possible. The key is to save as much as you can, from a very young age, so that you can retire when you want, and have financial solvency.

Factors to take into account when planning your retirement the right way

Making the decision to organize your retirement should be approached taking into account determining factors to cover the lifestyle you want to enjoy in your retirement.

Time

The main factor to take into account is time, that is when you plan to retire. The earlier you do this, the higher your fund will be and the better your quality of life will be.

Saving capacity

To build the savings fund you need, you must know your ability to save - the amount you have available monthly for your retirement plan.

Planning

Planning is the basis for organizing a successful retreat.

If you're 50 and still not planning for your retirement, you don't have to worry, you still have about 10 to 15 years to save. Even if you have 3 years left for retirement, you can plan and ensure your old age. It's a good idea to start right away and set up a plan to retire wisely.

Chapter 2
Main obstacles on the road to economic independence for the retirement stage

Lack of financial education

People avoid planning for retirement because they don't know the process for doing so. It is necessary to seek advice from qualified people, take management courses and know the process to manage their finances, to reduce risks.

Little capacity to save

It's the main reason why people are afraid to start planning their retirement. Thinking that they will not be able to cover other necessities of life, leads the person to postpone saving for their retirement plan.

Multiple obligations and commitments limit the savings capacity and make it difficult to increase the funds for old age.

Forgot to review your retirement plan

Retirement plans are long-term plans and require periodic review, as any event that occurs in your life affects your finances and savings capacity, thus affecting your investment strategy.

Financial responsibilities

Choose a responsible institution that guarantees good dividends. Choose appropriate government and private schemes that guarantee a good return on your savings.

Inflation

Every day the prices of the items go up and the money you planned today is not enough to buy the goods tomorrow. A smart savings plan meets your needs and avoids the headaches of being insolvent.

Inflation can affect your most basic needs, such as food, health, etc. If you start saving early, you can set up a savings fund enough to be safe from the effects of inflation.

Estimate life expectancy

It's a good idea to target a large amount for retirement, so that the retirement fund you've formed lasts long enough to support you for life and resists the onslaught of inflation.

Many people plan their retirement savings until a certain time and face problems because their age makes it difficult for them to work and generate income to meet their needs.

Financial intermediaries

Financial intermediaries generally keep a percentage of your dividends and decrease your savings fund, and the benefits are usually smaller. Deal directly with financial institutions, research the dividends your money will earn, and avoid intermediaries.

When you buy term life policies

It's important to know exactly how long you'll need the policy, so you don't overpay. For example: if you estimate that in 10 years you will be able to pay for your home, and you buy a fixed term life insurance for those 10 years, however, you could not pay your mortgage in that period of time, when you renew the fixed term life policy, the cost of the new insurance will be very high.

A realistic assessment should be made at the time you plan for retirement and purchase a life insurance policy.

Another reality you must face is that you may become ill and not be able to access a term life policy.

Mental

The main obstacle is fear, people deny the reality that they are going to grow old, and they must prepare for it. New responsibilities, thinking about investing, and feeling that you are no longer useful to society, become a mental block and end up postponing your retirement planning.

Fear is natural, we all feel it, but when it comes to the retirement stage, you must act safely, because it is the quality of life that is at risk, and if you cannot do it alone, you should seek help from professionals.

Chapter 3
Building Family Support for the Retirement Plan

The formation of values in the family is a great support for people who retire from their jobs, as it facilitates the transition from a working life to a new way of living. Are you wondering what values and family have to do with your retirement plan?

It is essential to have an empowered and committed team, willing to collaborate when needed. Implement practices that foster respect, solidarity, understanding, collaboration, and discipline so you have people to whom you can delegate, avoid stress, and feel overwhelmed.

The family can also contribute to saving for the retirement plan by avoiding unnecessary expenses, contributing a share of money to increase the retirement savings fund, and providing moral support.

The people closest to you are of great inspiration, to fight for the conquest of your dreams. They make you feel motivated and empowered in the face of challenges in this new stage of life.

A family group with strong bonds of union and love will make the retired person feel motivated to start a new life, with a positive mind and greater security.

Chapter 4
How do you gain financial independence to enjoy retirement?

There are many ways to achieve financial independence. Mainly, savings is the basis for investment and long-term planning. If you are a person thinking about protecting yourself from inflation, continuing the lifestyle you have while working or improving your quality of life, you can make other investments to increase your savings fund.

If your retirement savings fund depends solely on your salary, you may find yourself in serious financial trouble in your golden years.

According to specialists in the matter, the following strategies help to obtain financial independence for the enjoyment of a retirement, without worries for lack of money.

Don't underestimate how quickly you can grow your body or nest for retirement, even if you think it's too late.

Free Yourself from Debt

Pay off your debts, make an effort and pay for everything, big or small, and avoid contracting new ones. According to recent studies, some of the most common debts of Americans, ages 56 to 61, are:

— Private Loans

— Vehicle credits

— Mortgages

— Credit cards

Choose a strategy to pay your mortgage

Prioritize the payment of the most important debt; the mortgage. If your retirement is 10 years away, it should be your priority.

If you have more than 10 years left to retire, you can pay off your mortgage as you set out at the beginning and focus on other investments that will bring you immediate earnings and pay off your debts. Surely, the potential returns on your investment will be greater than the interest and it will become easier to reduce the mortgage debt. The deduction of interest from the mortgage is a tax benefit that will be useful in your working years. Consider a reverse mortgage.

Create a spending plan

Consider adjusting your expenses to the amount you will receive from the savings fund, making sure that the fund you are planning will cover your lifestyle.

Consider annual expenses to get closer to reality and consider the return on your retirement savings.

Retire Gradually

It is an option that tends to increase in the United States, seeing that you can barely live with retirement funds, to avoid remorse. More and more people are deciding to retire gradually, following these recommendations:

*Become a valuable and irreplaceable employee. Businesses need trusted employees. Being an outstanding employee makes you a key employee.

*Work part-time within the company. If you are a key employee, there will always be a place where you can contribute your knowledge within the organization.

*Find a reason for the employer to value your skills and hire you part-time. For example, if you have been a top sales manager for 35 years, you can take on the role of sales group coach for the company.

*Work remotely or part-time for the company.

Don't trust social security to cover all your needs

A quarter of the U.S. working population is planning 90% Social Security for retirement. The average monthly payment, estimated at $1,400, is insufficient to live in dignity, and seniors spend their retirement years struggling to survive.

One strategy is to increase the retirement age

For greater security in the last stage of their lives. For example, if you bring your social security bill forward to age 70, then you will receive 30% more than you would receive at standard retirement age.

Buy life insurance

Life insurance, in addition to paying for the insured's disability and death, has the option of covering expenses caused by serious illness and dependency.

The most common are:

Term Life Insurance

It is the most popular to have protection for a certain time, either, because your children are small and you need to make more expenses, you have a mortgage, or to meet needs until you have savings.

It is the simplest of all; the insured chooses an amount of coverage and defines the years he wants to keep the policy. If the needs no longer exist, you are free to choose whether or not to renew the insurance, saving premiums. This insurance allows you to keep your family well-off and also pay for your retirement fund.

Another advantage of these insurances is the price, since you are only buying for a certain time, and the premiums are exactly for the time that the insurer will cover your policy, without extra payments.

Term life insurance can be taken out for periods of one year or five and can be renewable. Also for 10, 15, 20 and 30 years, and the age to contract must be between 65 and 70 years.

The disadvantage of these policies is that if you did not estimate the correct time and purchased a policy of 20 years, to cover a specific need, and at the expiration date you have not been able to solve your situation, at the time of renewing the policy, you must pay the current price.

Level Term Insurance

The main feature of these policies is that they maintain the benefit of death during the life of the policy, and the insured amount does not change over time. **Fixed term life insurance** has the same characteristics as the previous one. They can expire or continue according to the option you choose, and which best suits your needs.

At the expiration of the **fixed term life insurance policy**, it can be continued for consecutive annual periods. Most of these policies allow you to renew your 90 years old coverage up to 100 years old.

Another form of level life insurance is that the person has the option of converting it into a permanent life insurance policy.

Renewable Term Life Insurance

With this life insurance, you have the right to extend the policy, unconditionally, without showing good health, for another period. The most common term is one year, they are offered to groups, through the employer as a company. It increases with each renewal and there may be restrictions for older ages.

Renewable term life insurance represents real savings on testing and ensures eligibility, however as time goes by its cost increases.

For example: A policy for a 65-year-old woman is more expensive than for a 25-year-old woman, both being in excellent health, and if you choose a 5-year renewable policy, you will pay less than if you choose a 30-year term policy.

It is important to keep in touch with the employer in order to know the benefits of this policy after the employment relationship ends.

Convertible Term Life Insurance

An insurance contracted for a temporary solution, and which can become a life insurance with permanent coverage, if you wish.

Permanent Life Insurance

These policies offer:

– Money Accumulation Value Guarantee

– Life insurance

– Adjustable and flexible death benefits, as you can increase or decrease within limits

– Accumulation of cash values

– Availability of additional cash value

A policy with premium refund

It is a novel premium, which pays back the money paid in premiums if you have not used it, it is alive, and the beneficiaries have not been benefited.

Declining Life Insurance

They are called declining because their financial means cover insurance needs, which young professionals cannot cover.

**To increase your income, you can invest in private savings plans, buy retirement insurance policies, invest in real estate, etc.

Chapter 5
How to develop a savings plan for retirement

The decision to develop a retirement plan includes some variables and, along with them, eliminate unclear "what if" thinking.

It's important to be clear about what lifestyle you're going to lead, if you're thinking about an expensive lifestyle, develop a more sophisticated plan. The following are tips that I would do myself and at no time should be taken as advice because each case is very particular and should be addressed as such.

Be honest with yourself and work out your retirement plan. This should be handwritten first, and contain the following elements:

Savings plan

Studying the strategy that will allow you to obtain the greatest benefits. While you are working, you can invest in other income-generating activities to make a greater contribution to your retirement plan. These activities allow you to better enjoy the new stage of your life and have the financial freedom you desire.

A middle-class professional invested 55% of his income in savings plans. Over the past 19 years, your account has grown at 12% per year. His interest grew every 6 years and he couldn't touch the funds. At first, you don't see the return, but as time goes by, you begin to see excellent results. With this strategy you can retire with a 19-year savings fund.

Professionals who can save 75% of their income can retire with a savings fund of 7 or 8 years.

Obviously, if you are earning 100 million, it will be easier to allocate 50% for your savings plan.

Now, it's really hard to save that percentage if you contribute only the money from your salary to the retirement savings fund, and you have a lot of obligations.

In order to elaborate a successful retirement plan, you must take into account the following aspects:

- What is your income?
- What are you going to do when you retire?
- What are your commitments?
- Consider lifestyle decisions
- Focus on the most important things in your life

If you are a salaried worker

- The job you have makes you feel comfortable, and you consider it well paid
- When do you plan to retire?
- How much should you contribute to the savings for the retirement plan?
- Can you contribute additional amounts to your retirement plan?
- The number of years you have to build it
- Calculate the savings fund you need for the time of your retirement, according to your life expectancy

If you are self-employed

- What do you currently have?
- How do you define an amount for your retirement fund?
- How many years do you have left to save?

What money do you need to build the retirement fund?

Some specialists say that to build a savings fund that guarantees a financially solvent, worry-free retirement life, a contribution of 10 times your annual monthly income is required.

Others recommend saving to replace 80% of annual income. It's all going to depend on the lifestyle you and your family have.

This sum indicates that you must think of other factors for a retirement that offers you a good quality of life since while working; you have obligations that logically do not allow you to assume this commitment of saving for retirement.

How to generate additional income and increase the contribution to your retirement savings fund?

Diversify your income

The more sources of income you have, the more likely you are to have solvency in your retirement. Among the best options are:

Start an online business generating passive income.

- Invest in real estate
- Invest in assets; buy commercial cars, rental machines, etc.
- Work part-time
- Transferring your savings account to a retirement plan is a good option

Investment Options

- Long-term savings plans
- Retirement plans
- Retirement insurance policies, you can buy as many as you want.
- Term Life Coverage
- Make investments and associate in businesses that generate dividends and cover expenses according to the lifestyle you have chosen

There are two ways to plan your retirement

The main thing is to start very early and define what life you want to live in your retirement and start planning. Your lifestyle defines your retirement plan.

1. If you want to live in a modest house, taking care of your garden, your grandchildren and enjoying the sunrise, it is possible that with only the government-employer retirement plan, you can survive.

2. If you really want to have a solvent retirement, where you can enjoy your years of life, be free of worries about paying your obligations, live a comfortable financial life, cover your expenses and those of your family, you must think about investing intelligently for old age.

It is important to take into account factors such as inflation, the savings fund you want to create and life expectations. You can estimate spending 4% per year of your retirement fund, and thus, this can last up to 25 years. It is recommended to save as much as you can. It's better to overdo it than to be left to your own devices.

Plan to build a retirement fund in 3 years

Although it may seem impossible, it can be achieved by diversifying income. A worker who plans his retirement at the beginning of his working life, but also begins to make investments and generate passive income, is likely to achieve a successful retirement plan in just 3 years.

The savings fund should cover 100% or more of your income.

The key is saving:

Setting priorities and saving

- To have an employer's retirement fund, in which the employer and employee contribute.

- Buy private retirement savings plans.

- After paying taxes, allocate no less than 20% to the savings fund. You can save according to your capacity, the more money you can save, the more economic solvency you will have in your retirement. Logically, if you want a sufficient retirement fund, in just 3 years, you must contribute more than 100% of your income.

— Today, technology has made it easier to enter online businesses. Anyone of any age can start a business and be very successful. On the net, you can start with very little capital and generate a lot of additional money. The business options are endless; you can buy, sell, monetize sites, among other options and generate income.

- Associating in small businesses generates dividends. The more investments you have, the more money you get, and you can have a better lifestyle. No matter how small the business, in the end, this passive income takes very little time out of your life and will be credited monthly to your bank account.

- You can also take a job that you can do remotely, in a short time and that generates an extra income.

- Have a savings account and invest in fixed assets, for commercial purposes, a car to provide taxi services, a bus for tourism services, a house to rent, tools or machinery to rent, etc.

- Reduce taxes, generating extra money for your retirement, after all, if you have children, they may live independently

— Sell those properties that you think you won't need and that will help you increase your savings fund.

You can plan your retirement in 3 years; however, you should make an effort to save and choose the best plan that you think is convenient and enjoy your retirement.

Activity Plan

Date / Activity	Mon	Tues	Wed	Thurs	Fri	Sat	Sun
Usual							
Special							

How to set goals for a successful retirement plan?

Each of the steps you must take to complete your retirement plan is an objective, and each of these small steps brings you closer to the goal of fully enjoying your retirement plan.

In the retirement savings plan, you should list each of your goals, in a systematic and disciplined manner, to form a retirement savings fund that will ensure your financial solvency.

They should be clearly stated, written in an affirmative tone that leaves no room for doubt. Contain clear data such as the place, date, activity, who is involved and what you want to achieve.

Evaluate each activity, the development and performance of your money; remember that the product of a successful plan is your welfare.

Change of habits

- Avoid spending money on unnecessary things
- Be organized and disciplined
- Control compulsive shopping
- Avoid the use of credit cards
- Avoid unnecessary indebtedness
- Avoid procrastination
- Eat healthily
- Prepare your own food; it's a way to stay healthy and save money
- Establish a standard of quality, price, and quantity in your personal items
- Take care of your health
- Avoid stress

– Delegate functions

It is not a question of living a precarious life; on the contrary, it is important to spend money consciously and intelligently, ensuring a better quality of life.

Schedule of activities

Create a calendar of activities where each of the small steps or goals that will lead you on the safe path to retirement and comfortable financial freedom are established.

Schedule of activities

Activity / Date Time	Appt. with the accountant	Attend the administration course	Go to the bank to open a savings account	Visit the insurance comp.	Accomplished Yes	Accomplished No	Responsible

Chapter 6
Investment Strategy

Financial security is not a matter of chance; it requires planning and commitment, which will be successful if applied with the necessary knowledge.

When to start saving?

Right now, if you haven't started, do it now.

U.S. private industry offers its workers defined contribution plans, yet there is little on the workers' side to know how it works.

Start as soon as possible and try to increase the percentage of savings each month. Make retirement savings a priority. Do it through a well-structured plan.

Know Your Retirement Needs

It is important to take into account inflation, and the difficulty it produces in maintaining a lifestyle similar to the one you had in early retirement. Experts affirm that you will need 70 - 90% of the salary you received when you were still working, to cover expenses in your retirement.

If your employer offers you a retirement plan, such as the famous 401(k), take it because it pays less tax, and it's done automatically, making things easier for you. Compound interest and tax deferral are beneficial to your retirement plan.

Set the time, whether it's 5, 15, 25 or 35 years.

Find out how much your retirement savings contribution should be to get the fund you're looking to raise.

Calculate, according to the periods above, if you have saved $5,500 each year, and your money earns 7% annually, how much is the amount saved at the end?

Are you worried about researching how the retirement plan works? What happens if you change jobs? Value of your savings and benefits. Ask all the questions you consider pertinent to have a clear vision about your financial future. Put all your savings into different types of investments.

Diversification brings a return on your savings and reduces risks. Empower yourself with knowledge, and keep in mind that financial security goes hand in hand with knowledge.

Don't have the savings and retirement funds to cover other matters, on the contrary, contribute to the fund as much as possible. Avoid fines, earn taxes and interest and make your money grow.

If you change jobs, transfer retirement funds to your new employer's plan. If your employer doesn't offer it, continue to pay individually or start one. The important thing is not to stop saving.

For Individual Retirement Accounts (IRAs), you can start with $5,500 or less a year. You can contribute more if you're over 50, so you can build a larger retirement fund. The tax benefits of IRA accounts will depend on the plan you have chosen.

Look for information about your social security; they usually pay 40% of what you earned in pre-retirement. If you're a woman, ask questions about any changes in your retirement savings plan.

Try to invest and generate passive income to increase your savings fund.

Maintain communication with your employer, union, financial partners and advisors. Ask questions and make sure you understand them well.

*If you don't know the subject, don't have time, or think it's a little complicated to understand, seek the advice of qualified personnel.

Chapter 7
Mental preparation for a new stage in your life

To make decisions in life requires mental clarity, to know where you're going and how to do it. Mental clarity is achieved with the firm decision, will and knowledge to do things, a product of the knowledge you have of yourself.

The elderly person in addition to thinking of new challenges that are approaching his life, presents a kind of nostalgia to leave behind, which was his workplace for many years and must adapt to this new reality.

Fortunately, the human mind can exercise regardless of age. It is important that your thoughts match your actions and words. Some mental exercises to have a clear mind and send a clear message to your subconscious mind are:

- Visualize through mental images the person you want to become.

- Believe that you are able to lead a productive and financially comfortable life. Achieve all your goals and give your group or family a good quality of life.

- Maintain a positive attitude that attracts prosperity and success in your projects.

- Feel gratitude for what you have achieved, for having passed a stage of your life and begin to enjoy your efforts throughout the years of work.

- Connect often with your inner self and review those things that have always caught your attention and that you would like to do. It's the right time to fulfill your dreams. You have the time you haven't had before if you plan your retirement wisely, you have the money to make it happen.

- No matter how old you are, people don't know themselves. The lack of self-knowledge becomes fears, insecurities and low self-esteem, which is reflected by mental blocks, which do not allow you to see clearly and make good decisions.

- Work constantly inside yourself and strengthen your mind, so that you can make the right decisions and achieve the welfare you hoped to experience so much.

There are relaxation exercises that can help you manage emotions, especially in the golden years when you feel nostalgia for what is behind you, depression at the thought that you have failed, or don't know how to face new challenges. These exercises are Mindfulness Meditation, Yoga, and Tai Chi, among others.

New challenges

You must be mentally prepared to face new challenges in retirement. Many people are content to take care of grandchildren and watch television, promoting the culture of leisure. However, the retiree must remain active and participate in cultural activities in order to face a physically, mentally, and emotionally healthy retirement.

Chapter 8
A 7-step system to end your procrastination in retirement planning

– Avoid procrastination of retirement savings and act immediately, the sooner you start saving, the better.

– Define the life you want to enjoy in your old age. This is a topic you should discuss with your family.

– Seek guidance from people with experience in the topic of finance.

– Take control and take a course in accounting.

– Thoroughly review investment options in different financial institutions.

– Research the features and benefits of your employer's retirement plan.

– Reduce your expenses and increase your income.

Chapter 9
10 tips to get one financially stable

Today, thanks to technological advances, it is possible to know the characteristics, retirement savings plans and benefits offered by different government and private institutions, for a choice that meets your expectations and ensures a successful retirement.

Tips to get a financially stable retirement plan:

- Use technology to get information about each savings and retirement plan.
- Use the retirement estimator on the Social Security website.
- Choose the plan that offers you the best tax advantages.
- Try to set up your account so that the amount is automatically deducted from your checking or savings account.
- Ask questions about investment plans and options.
- Check to see if the employer's pension plan covers the plan and show interest in how it works, and the value of your benefit.
- Find out if your spouse's plan benefits you.
- Choose the plan that offers the most benefits, pays the least taxes and is easy to manage.
- Count on the help of a financial analyst to choose the plan that fits the lifestyle you want to enjoy at this stage of your life.
- Choose an institution that has the technological resources to project your needs, based on the asset-liability ratio.

Chapter 10
10 gaps to avoid in preparation for retirement

- **Refuse training to plan a retirement savings plan**

The most difficult obstacle to learning is when the person believes that he knows everything and refuses to receive instructions from another. In the process of planning for retirement, it is of utmost importance to receive information to improve knowledge in finance. Remember that your peace of mind and that of your family depend on how effectively you manage your resources.

- **Trust only government and employer retirement allocation rules.**

It is not enough to live an economically comfortable life and the more investments you make, the greater your income and possibilities to increase your retirement fund and ensure a better future.

- **Save only on IRAs and 401(k)s**

It is important to have these retirement plans; however, it is advisable to have other savings and investment options to improve your financial capacity.

- **Think that only with dividends, you can cover your retirement expenses**

It is advisable to diversify investments, the more sources of income you have, the more benefits you get.

- **Avoid looking for other investment options and invest only in stocks and bonds.**

You should be predictive and take into account factors such as inflation, falling prices in stocks and bonds. For this reason, it is important to have other investments to help you maintain your status when your stocks and bonds have declined.

- **Start saving for retirement at the last minute**

Time is the only time that guarantees a sufficient accumulation of wealth to fully enjoy your old age. Start planning and saving at a very young age and ensure financial solvency for your retirement.

- **Choosing a savings plan without having studied other options**

Many times, due to lack of time, ignorance or disinterest, people take the plans they are first offered, and they lament at the end, when it is late and realize that they are retired and forced to work to survive.

- **Choose a retirement plan and forget to review it periodically**

It is important that you periodically review the performance of your money, taking advantage of benefits and incentives that could offer in a given time. Remember that only you decide about your money.

- **Taking money from the retirement fund for other expenses**

Lack of organization and financial discipline leads to an imbalance in your finances. Taking money from your retirement for other purposes is a mistake that many people make, effective planning, assisted by professionals could avoid these cases.

You lose capital and interest, plus the benefit of taxes and retirement penalties.

- **Fear of investing**

Fear is an obstacle that stops you and does not allow you to advance, affecting the emotional and economic stability of you and your family. The more investments you can make, the better your quality of life will be.

Conclusion

Planning and saving go hand in hand to face intelligently the moment when you have to give up your life's work. The system in which we live prepares us to be productive, to develop as people within society and to contribute to the development of the country. However, many times the parties involved leave aside the responsibility of informing workers in a timely manner about the different options they have to choose a retirement savings plan that guarantees the enjoyment of their retirement years.

After the Second World War, we observed that social security became personal security. Although some assert that it is the responsibility of government and employers to advise individuals to make the best financial decision. Each individual must ensure their safety, evaluate and plan for the life they want to enjoy after retirement, and have a financial institution that guarantees a good return and benefits on their dividends.

The problem is that retirees are not doing enough to ensure a dignified and successful financial retirement. The right thing is to enjoy the wonders of life, after long hours of work and effort, for many years. Rescue a little of what we have lost by being limited by long hours of work and most importantly, being closer and sharing with your family.

Time is a determining factor in planning a better quality of life for the retired person. The more time you have to retire, the more possibilities you have to increase your retirement fund, with which to cover basic health, housing, and education needs. Planning ahead guarantees a dignified and stable retirement. Retirees can work if they wish, but not out of necessity.

It is worth making a small effort to generate extra income and place it in the retirement savings fund, we well know that the older you get the less chance you have of obtaining credit and life insurance becomes more expensive.

The smart way to ensure a happy old age is to take advantage of your youth and save as much as you can, only then, in your golden years you won't have to stress about work. The ideal is to retire thinking that you are going to rest, be at home with your children or grandchildren, and enjoy nature, travel, and study if you wish, without thinking about financial limitations and feeling free because you have finally freed yourself from the stress caused by work.

www.ingramcontent.com/pod-product-compliance
Lightning Source LLC
Chambersburg PA
CBHW040301220526
45473CB00002B/548